Spiritual Gait

Steven J. Jacobson

ISBN 978-0-692-21357-5
Cover photo: thinkstockphotos.com
Cover Design: Cornerstone Copy Center

Library of Congress Cataloging –in-Publication-Data

Jacobson, Steven Jeffrey.
spiritual gait: poems / Steven Jeffrey Jacobson.

ISBN 978-0-692-21357-5
70# white paper

Cornerstone Copy Center
13775 Frontier Court
Burnsville, MN 55337

Spiritual Gait

Acknowledgments

The author wishes to thank the editors of the following publications in which these poems were previously published, occasionally with a different title or in a different version:

"Watery Dwelling", Access Press, Volume 19 No.5 (May 10, 2008), Page 7

"Cherub-Child", Calvary Cross, (April 30, 2013), Page 1

"Abounding Child", "Light N' Life" and "Light of Gold", Calvary Cross, (May 3, 2013), Page 1

"Ocean's Alive", Linnet's Wings, (June 29, 2013), Summer, Page 64 (Copy rights revert back after September 30, 2013)

"Coffee for Two", Burningword Literary Journal, (July 1, 2013), Summer Issue 67, Page 74

"Wetlands", The Glass Coin, (July 18, 2013), Summer, Page 1

"Light of Gold", "Cherub-Child", "A Child, God's Gift", "Child Yearning for Love", "Love N' Life" and "Spring and the Eternal Friend" Anthology, Love Unconditionally (theme) Metric Conversions, metreli kaytarmalar (Aug 7, 2013), Page 125-137, ISBN 978-60662 44497   Note: Cherub-Child and Light of Gold first published by Calvary Cross (April and May 2013)

"Earthscape", The Glass Coin, (Aug 8, 2013), Summer, Page 1

"Homeward Bound" and "Abounding Child", Praise Writer, (Aug 16, 2013), Issue 2, Page 10. Note: Abounding Child first published by Calvary Cross (May 2013) (Copy rights revert back after Feb 16, 2014 on individual poems)

"Coffee for Two", Eunoia Review, (Sept 16, 2013), Fall, Page 1. Note: Coffee for Two first published by Burningword Literary Journal, (2013) "Reprinted with the permission of Burningword Literary Journal and the author[s]."

"Color the Earth", Penwood Review, (Fall 2013), Volume 17, Number 2, Page 37

"Criss-cross", Little Red Tree Publishing, Anthology, Fall 2013, Page 44-45.

"Earth-scape" and "Watery Dwelling", Message in a Bottle, (Spring 2014), Note: Earth-scape was first published by Gold Coin (Aug 2013), and Watery Dwelling was first published by Access Press (May 2008)

Heartfelt thanks for Marcia Thompson Jacobson and Susan D. Jacobson for editing the book of poetry. And for Susan Dahlby and Cindy Goustin for their support and amazing skills. Special thanks to Kaposia Inc. for supporting my work and providing a grant making this a dream come true.

CONTENTS

I Nature Calling

CONTENTS

CONTENTS

III   Child Escapades

CONTENTS

IV Earthly Encounters

CONTENTS

V Spiritual Endeavors

Spiritual Gait

I

NATURE CALLING

"And when I was born, I drew in the common air,
and fell upon the earth, which is of like nature;
and the first voice which I uttered was crying,
as all others do."

-Solomon Ibn Gabirol

Spring and the Eternal Friend

spring is a flower beginning to bloom
as the sun rises above the earth
in golden rays of light. life begins to flow
through the veins of the world signifying
a new day has arisen. friendship is the union
between souls desperately seeking
beauty and love, which transcends
and bridges a void within the world
of co-existence. friendship, like spring,
blossoms fourfold, growing and fulfilling
one's heart's desire and letting us not forget,
we are in debt to our God for those relationships and
the unconditional love given to each of us.

Rebirth of the Soul

the days are filled with heart rendering
songs of praise to our God, as the
flowers blossom, the woodlands flourish and
the waters become a majestic hue.
the fragrance in the breeze testifies
to the rebirth of the human spirit,
as the golden fiery orb fills the earth
with sunlight. the fertile lands spurt forth
green vegetation as they pay homage to our King.
fruit springs from the inner recesses of love as
God's ordained plan unfolds.

Color the Earth

the season unreels with an air of majesty
and mystery measured by God's celestial clock.
the world witnesses the changing times,
as the air becomes cool and crisp.
the colors: reds, oranges, yellows and mixed colors
mark the leaves, a testament to the beautiful
labor of love manifested in nature.
the colors fill the spectrum of the senses and
shine in the hearts of all who survey
God's work. the leaves labor to
maintain their life flowing force
only to be swept away by the wind and rain,
returning to the earthen soil from whence they
came.

Winter's Haven

snowflakes fall deftly
as the angelic moon glows,
silhouetting the open woodlands
far beneath the enlightening sky.
the ground glistens and crackles
under the soft padding of creatures
scurrying in the night, as it hides their
nocturnal activities and playfulness.
the stars pulse and project an orchestral
ensemble of peace and tranquility playing out
over God's given earth.

Wetlands

spring-time brings willows blooming
in the marshes, skirting the shallow shoreline.
small game: swallows, gulls, finches and
black-birds harbor among wispy yellow-green
shoots and reeds and young spindly ferns and firs.
smaller vegetation of dandelions and
grass weaves a velvety tapestry on the outskirts.
an eagle takes off, soaring effortlessly overhead.
the billowy white clouds kaleidoscope
against the blue sky from moment to precious
moment. the breeze, gusty winds and sunshine
exchange voices, complementing and completing
the perfect picture in time and space.

Homeward Bound

millennia pass and the waters flow melodically
on an epic sojourn as a testimony to our Creator.
the channel widens, gathering speed and resolution,
polishing and recreating stones of ivory.
the torrent stream cascades downward in a
swirling and spiraling display of wonderment
manifested by our God. time is captured by all
who perceive the enchantment spun by our senses.
the white-caps swell and heave in effortless force,
as they recombine in frothy resonance.
the turbulence recedes and becomes tranquil
on the journey home.

Ocean's Alive

the emerald sea washes against the jagged
rocks in continuous attempts to crash and
display a mighty show of force while
polishing and smoothing the craggy shoreline.
the air tastes of saltiness and the sea gulls
rampage the sky circling for morsels
of food. the golden fiery orb bears down
while a gentle breeze offers a reprieve from the
heat. a myriad of sunken footprints covers the
beach, littered with sea shells and small crabs.
while the tide ebbs, life is measured and realized to
be precious and worthy of special regard.

Nostalgia

the woodlands beckon to peacefulness and serenity
abounding in the wild. the music, emulating from
the fowl and the animals, flows like molasses in a
summer breeze. greenery and vegetation
encapsulate and lift the soul by revealing a portrait
of enduring beauty. time passes silently and
longingly while invigorating the senses. nature's
path weaves and ensconces, revealing the spectrum
of life newly reborn.

Wonderland Revisited

dawn approaches with etchings of glorious hues,
transcribed by the golden orb and earth's
atmosphere. the sunlight displays
a curtain of rays dancing on the horizon
while manifesting an aura of radiance and splendor.
the colors shower and reel the senses; a
semblance of wonder is created for earth and
for heaven. majesty and beauty project outwardly
to the eye of the beholder. the day progresses
forward enveloped by newness and freshness,
while the sun unfolds a delightful dream-like
peacefulness for mankind.

Light N' Dark

the red rose dances timidly and triumphantly,
transforming into a radiant and resounding sunset,
blossoming into fullness and blessing,
being as one living with a love for life.
petals magically and mysteriously open outwardly,
offering the onlooker and the world
meaningful moments for the mindfulness.
the stem embraces the delicate flower while
disarmingly pointed thorns greet the
bold ones with penetrating pain and poignant
memories. the rose carries a dual message to the world,
conveying both light and darkness, co-existing in the
realm of nature.

Clouds N' Stuff

the clouds carry
their vaporous wispiness, bending
and twisting but always changing like
a grouping of flowering white roses reaching
fullness and bloom. the heavens graciously
open wide and shine forth in their splendor,
bounty and blazing glory.
beckoning to all a new vision
and view of life's possibilities,
as time and space enters into these
miniscule magical moments of life.

Spiraling Upward

centuries have given way to millennia for the
great icons of the sky. the young sapling
changes to a hearty and steadfast fir
as the seasons pass by.

the boughs and branches intertwine
and cross each other in a maze of
glory. the roots collectively
portray a mirror image underground.

the bourgeoning leaves yearn for
life and regeneration freely given by
Our God. seeds spew forth and the circle
of life is reborn.

Reach for the Sky

the vaporous silhouettes gleam true to the glorious
imbued qualities given by God. the shapeless
forces of nature transform and inspire works of art
as witnessed by heaven and earth.
the bountiful, billowy and fluffy ice crystals
glide through the air on a heavenly carpet.
celestial trumpets and holy harps resound and play
melodic notes praising God.
the colors emulate the spectrum of visual patterns
combined with sunshine and
enclosed by blue sky. repetition is a myth
but beauty is eternal.

Nature's Playground

a wooden glider rocks gently
in motion. thoughts
drift outward beyond the self
and engulf Mother Nature.
time transforms rhythms and
melodic notes, reeling the soul to a
whirlwind of excitement. the sky
turns summersaults and the ground
heaves upward. the sun flits by like
a pendulum on a golden string.
the peak of the free fare induces
amazement; propelling one to soar on
wings of eagles, ever higher and higher
into the yonder blue.

Moon Struck

the white disc glistens and glows
filling the world with a sublime light
perched in the night-time sky.
the moon shines over the lake and
trees, playing with the clouds in hide
and seek fashion as the orb heads
for the horizon. moonbeams dapple
and touch upon the window shade and pane.
at the break of dawn, dark undertones score
the shade and sill from the vegetation
nearby.

Night N' Gale

the disturbance grows dark and growls.
lightning laces the sky
unleashing fury and force.
embers burning, timber stripped away
the grass is smoldering and animals are scurrying.
vacuum collapsing, a mighty rush,
thunder explodes shaking the ground, the sound
echoes in the distance as dawn approaches.
the gales roar and gnarl,
the rains come in droves,
followed with gentle shower.
a rainbow appears, God's promise,
the birds and animals return.
all is peaceful once more.

Storm N' Shine

the evolving and earthen soil is carved and
carried away by continuous streams
cascading from the cumulus-nimbus
thunder clouds overhead. the thunderstorms
lace the sky with surreal light and clashing
sounds like cymbals crashing in the distance.
the rain races and rivets the ground with
disheveling droplets, dispersing randomly
round the rich and receiving soil. the ground
dances and dreams of this moment and measures
where it plays with the rain. the sun glows and
glistens as it is called upon to shine, displaying a
radiant and vibrant rainbow; God's promise to
His creation.

II

LOVE AND LIVE

"To love for the sake of being loved is human, but to love for the sake of loving is angelic."

-Alphonse de Lamartine

Blossoming Love on Mother's Day

on this momentous occasion,
memories arise as untold stories of love and joy,
abounding in truth and harmony from
our God above. the flowers offering
their beauty and brilliance
as the colors and bouquet awaken
during a glorious and spellbinding sunrise.
to all partaking, there manifests a song
of praise and adoration to our Creator,
dispensing heavenly ecstasy which fills
the hearts on this special day.

Light of Gold

the sun reaches out with tendrils of
radiant splendor, stretches forth across
the heavens and redefines our world in
longing reverence. the light bursts
through the clouds, showers and adorns
the land and sea. the mountains and valleys
reflect and model the hues of the earth.
life is fruitful and full of wonder.
just as the sun shines in our faces,
so God wants His glory to shine in all
our hearts.

Heavenly Delight

the rapture experienced at first sight
envelops our emotions. the vision unfolds and
leaves a permanent etching in the heart. the beauty
displays God's work in all living things. the aroma
released by a bouquet of flowers transcends all
earthly pleasures, lighting up the senses and
intoxicating the soul. the spirit is transformed and
raised to commune with Mother Nature and the
Almighty God. the petals are velvet soft,
commanding an air of royalty and a touch of
heavenly delight. the pollen is regenerated on the
wings of the bumble bee and the circle of life begins
anew.

Weaver of Love

the days of summer touch on a romantic and
melodic chord of nature. love and
beauty flow through the arteries and veins
of the world. the magic of life refocuses and
touches the heart and soul of all who drink
deeply of the flowering nectar. living and
giving abound as the Tailor of life's tapestry
weaves his art. the love of life and the
life of love meld into one. peace and joy,
sharing and caring, reach out like many ripples;
joining one another in the pond of life
we connect with each other and God.

Jump In

the brilliant colors create a rainbow of
expectations in the eyes, soul and heart
of the onlooker. one has only to see from a
different perspective the beauty of the world meant
for everyone to enjoy. the child in all of us brings
his innocence and wonder to the enlivening
earth we share with one another and God.
the hues of flowers, trees,
woodlands, lakes and skies
nestle in hearts with love mingled
between ourselves and God.
enjoyment comes from loving
and living in the indescribable moments
connected to one another in the stream
of time and space.

Second Sight

the day moves forward, as do the beautiful
flowers like roses, tulips and lilacs
move with the breeze. the whimsical
nature of nature is how the flowers
color the ground as the bystander grounds
himself in the moment and drinks in
the surrounding nectar of life by
loving life. the truth hits one
as the truth is received from God.
the heart of the matter is how
opening the heart is coupled with
God's love and grace. in the spirit of giving,
God's Spirit mingles with
our spirit.

Light N' Life

the stars circle, spiraling
inwardly taking on new meaning
as the twilight fills the air.
a slice of randomness walks with
memorable stature and form.
we are forever mesmerized,
taking part in the grander
scheme offered up by light and dark.
the sun plays and dances,
a part of a deeper thought
and forever coupled with the
forthcoming of light and life.

Dawn's Moment

summertime is a free-for-all,
for all the avid 4th of July people.
wildlife attunes to the noise.
days segue toward the twilight realm as
the stars captivate the bystanders.
fireworks lace the sky with a deluge of
bombardments of bright flashing
forms and colored lights followed by
smoky trails of the burning embers.
the grand finale brightens the sky to an
early dawn for only a few moments.
the great exodus of the people follows
with the exception of the humming
and stinging native mosquito.

Love N' Life

summer evokes a spiritual journey as one
takes a walk through the woodlands and
open meadows as they approach a fresh water
stream. a connection to the animals
and earth ignites a fire of destiny as
heart, soul and mind meld with
love for life and life for love.
people demonstrate different ways to
live and love as nature changes
itself into a dream state of a personal
nature with our God and Creator.
the experience is transcendental and
transforming. sharing with one another
expressions of joy and peace as our
spiritual being resonates within
our temporal being.

Love's Harbor

the harbor to love's gate binds
the consciousness between hearts and souls to an
everlasting bond. love deepens and guides us
forward, growing and shaping into an
image of our Creator. God's love like
a light-house, is glowing, giving and providing
a lighted path. as we grow closer in kinship
by melding and becoming an enlivening spirit,
God's presence ferries us to a new body of water
and a new way to value ourselves and view life.
love's touch embraces, all encompassing while
measuring the transcendence of time and space.
the view is breath-taking and the horizon
spans an endless realm of the body of
water and possibilities of love's calling and
promising nature.

Love's Carousel

the carousel of love fosters and focuses,
becoming a circular flow of giving and
receiving. the sea and soil are blessed with
water droplets from the amassing thunder clouds
which release their bounty and booty to the earth.
the rain, part of the cycle, is freeing and furthering
life's bond. the cycle of love is like the parting
of clouds. the playfulness of the sunlight
beams and bounces around.
it is received by an unsuspecting bystander
who gives back by smiling and laughing like
being on a carousel of life.

Heaven Sent

the adventure awaiting mankind is to affirm and
accept life by appreciating life, absenting himself
from the tree of knowledge, attuning himself to
God's answers and amusing anecdotes in the living
bible. the truth is offered by our Savior Christ
Jesus. the open heart and the innocents of a child's
ways bring a breath-taking and bold view of the
good news. The good news, breaking and
blossoming belief, transcribes and witnesses to the
bystanders in word and action. the bold and brave
and brazen new world viewed through new eyes,
free to follow our course as freedom follows the
framework of our Father in Heaven.

Love N' Clouds

the obscure and opaque
nature of clouds offers a tantalizing
display of an open and direct season
to the heart. the clouds flow and gather like
the movement of the heartbeat,
growing and blossoming. love
transcends all understanding with the
human mind and tongue but bears
tribute and truth to translating and
believing. life of a cloud, like love,
changes and grows, gleaming true.
the heart, like the sun's rays,
offers an ever changing array
of cadence and color.

Law N' Love

the kindling knowledge carries a
cautionary clue, caught in living
life with one foot and leg in the
consuming fire. the law of the land
languishes while meaning to
measure and meter the
committed crimes
by weighing its method of dispensing justice.
the perplexing penalty to be
administered and applied fits
nothing less than physical death.
God's love is benevolent and
bountiful and surpasses all understanding.
His shining Son becomes flesh from
the word as in the beginning and
dwells among us. love is the cornerstone.
the body of Christ blossoms
and gives birth to amazing grace and truth,
where love overturns physical death for all
eternity.

Leap N' Live

how many of us are slowly sinking and
seeking less stress and more peace in
each of our segmented and shapeless days?
take a hint and do the leap into the pool of
refreshing water, rejuvenating our bodies,
hearts and spirits. the cool and sudden
stimulating transformation infuses our insides,
warming us up like a trip to a
tropical paradise with bountiful sunshine.
swimming is secondary, but we segue
into this simple routine without any
realization or suggestion from our fellowman.
submersing ourselves completely is like
reliving and reminding us of our baby
baptismal. the gift of God's love, mercy and
peace is like being born again,
witnessing and opening ourselves.
romancing the water in one's daily rigors of life is a
beautiful and breath-taking spiritually rewarding
journey.

Abounding Hope

the hope of tomorrow
transcends and extends
between both the good and
bad times of today. destiny
guides itself onward
past the here and now
but its reverse side,
free will, wakes in the present.
ascending to the truth,
through faith in life,
it fulfills one to abide
in God's love and grace
for all eternity.

Grateful to God

the morning time is a deluge of expectations and
wonder as the light of gold rises and spills its
rays and colors over the hills and valleys.
the connection to God is forever made, forever
united and forever realized in an instant in time
and space. these moments make up the reality
where light and truth are forever more.
God's love and grace are sufficient for all time
when realizing that time is only an illusion and
we are made in God's image.

God's Gift of Love

He was born into a dark world, overcoming the veil
of darkness. from the time we live life till we die,
there is a desire for self-worth and self-esteem by
seeking self-gratification and self-validation to
define who we are in the world. we see only the
limitations in ourselves until we value ourselves and
one another in the light of God's love and grace
and realize love and peace are forever.

III

CHILD ESCAPADES

"A thing of beauty is a joy forever: its loveliness increases; it will never pass into nothingness."

-John Keats

Cherub-Child

the being and birth
of the bethel-babe
share and shine like a new penny.
they circulate around and collect
the imagination and innocence of hearts
and harbor soul and spirit.
they charm and care for the
celestial cherub-like
connection and
partake, please and possess
our true disembodiment of spirit
from the physical mind and body.
their spirit effortlessly empties, endures
and endlessly overflows like a brimming brook.
God provides a safe haven and a sanctuary
for the weary while the throbbing and touching
tributaries of love and life are forever entwined.

Abounding Child

the body of a child,
vessel holding precious liquid.
the mind of a child,
an empty slate board.
the innocence of a child,
pure and golden.
the heart of a child,
overflowing carafe of vintage wine.
the soul of a child,
rich and resonating with love and laughter.
the spirit of a child,
soaring high with grace and glory abounding.
the love of a child,
pure driven snow covering a pristine landscape.
the life of a child,
ageless and free forever and ever......

White Flakes Falling

stars over stars, …

swirling amidst one another,
moving carefree with curious tongues reaching,
finding and touching treats. minds adrift under

stars over stars, …

soft laughter and telling tears bearing
creating and casting joy,
faces shaping and shining under

stars over stars,…

little boots crushing and crunching,
crinkling under the pressure of precious making
feet. marking memories from the spell under

stars over stars, …

silent twilight dusk descending,
covered ground covering
flurry found jackets, mittens and hats under

stars over stars …

Chance Encounter

the day groaned by at its usual pace…
all seemed in place.
an angel appeared…
life wasn't the same anymore.
you see, times being what they are,
with life's routines,
it just doesn't happen that way.
the moral of the story is just this;
isn't it great to be alive
sharing your life with another human being.

Burgeoning Sky

one enjoys the vaporous silhouettes, adorning and
      draping blue-turquoise sky and horizon.
the magnificent star plunges toward
      jagged rocky precipices.
a lone eagle races skyward,
      homeward bound.
the moon is perched on the horizon,
      gaining in brilliance as it rises.
setting glory,
      color of pomegranate,
growing sweeter, more intoxicating and vibrant
      reaching the core.
sunset is climatic, colors shining as
      drowning, reawakening.
the glassy sea surface
      mirrors crimson delight.
the sun plays off clouds
      as dusk overcomes twilight.
the stars are shining in firmaments,
      revealing the night time sky.

A Child: God's Gift

the innocence given by God
to a child remains a mystery
to the adult world.

the love unconditionally
expressed by a child to another
is unparalleled in this life.

the twinkle in the child's eyes
casts more light than all
the stars and galaxies combined.

the words uttered by a child
have more meaning than all
the knowledge of the world.

the truth mastered by a child
is simple yet far reaching
and is God's maxim to mankind.

Child Yearning for Love

child yearns for his mother's
embraces and endears himself like
a small ocean wave rises and crashes
upon the seashore and continually reaches out.
the beauty and bloom of a babe wrapped in a
blanket evolve and enliven to become
and behold. baby tries and toils
during the days that overlap the marvelous and
meaningful times to be one with his mother.
birthrights full of wonder exist between
each other. relationships transcend
the beautiful sunset in harmony
and communion with our God. beauty unfurls
and opens the way to everlasting love
for one another and the heart of the world.

Dream Cycle

the course of a river is not unlike
life. the stream winds and flows
over and around hills and valleys,
dictating the path but not the ride.
the sky is like our consciousness,
open and playful but only the tip
of the iceberg. our being is
awaiting to awaken and become
the core of our reality.
each of us is given a new chance
to dream and awaken to a new vision
coming into focus.

Shimmering Spirit

the wooly white flakes
whistling and whipping
through the winding and whirling.
the snow cleanses and creates a newness
like the newborn nature.
a vessel housing our spirit,
mingling and melding with God's Spirit.
Christmas cheer is
echoing and enchanting.
encompassing and enveloping,
growing and gaining.
a blowing and bombarding blizzard.
the storm is spreading and snow balling,
like the marriage of Spirit to spirit.
changing the coarseness of the world
through loving life and
life-giving love.

Esther-Virtuoso

eyes brightly lit and beaming like ten thousand
candles beckoning forth from a campfire.

mind eager and empathetic like
Sister Maria in the Sound of Music.

hands delicate and demure like a
virtuoso violinist playing at Carnegie Hall.

soul patient and pure like a vestibule and
virgin mountain stream.

hair jet black and bold like a raven
free to follow her course.

face awesome and appreciating like an avid
gymnast enthusiast enthralled with the Olympics.

heart beautiful and blossoming like a radiating
rose garden.

Micah N' Art

eyes bright and blue like the deep and
dreamy body of wealth.

hands and fingers harboring and focusing like a
colorful cartoon and sci-fi creator of amazing art.

face shining and smiling like a child's
first step forward into seeing nature.

soul mindful and mystic like the
creation of music from a great guitarist.

hair rich and radiant like the moon's luminescent
and lucent rays of light.

mind coaxing and caring like a father's
fostering love and riches for his child.

heart gentle and gracious like the white and
woolen clothing of a baby sheep.

Mark N' Music

eyes hazel and happening like the sun
shining upon the lazy and hazy lustrous sea.

hair dark and dapple like a sleek and
slender grayish-brown koala.

face glistening and gleaming like a true
troubadour facing a grateful crowd.

soul patient and pure like a diamond with
perfect cut, clarity and color.

smile friendly and forthright like the
beautiful and blazing sunshine.

hands welcoming and working like a musician
drifting with a God given talent, the guitarist.

heart rendering and reeling like a glowing and
glimmering sunrise.

IV

EARTH ENCOUNTERS

"Forget not that the earth delights to feel
your bare feet and the winds long to play
with your hair."

-Khalil Gibran

Criss-cross

sitting there like
stiff white coats and ties;
trying to jump-start the mind on things to do today.
thoughts of breakfast and personal cleanliness
come into consciousness
but quickly change to
contemplating the quietness of the hour.
the refrigerator's low hum sounds
and some hissing noise
remotely ensues from the apartment walls.
room vast like
revolving white wards of yester-year.
books covering the room
chanting, reach out and touch me.
oh how my heart yearns to reach out to the world.
stories spewing out like
people milling about aimlessly in the not so distant past.
plots swallowing me up like
white pills taken yesterday.
my thoughts refocus again,
hoping as a broken smile
to live in the present.
my soul still burns as a low lit candle,
deep and bright. clinging to the past reemerges
along with my two bailiwicks; my mental health
and loneliness and that damn hissing
sound off in the distance.

Death Visits Mikey And His Family

the snow
was falling deafly,
blanketing the ground
but indifferent
to the day.
unsuspecting and innocent
lay the slumbering forms
in a dwelling
on the outskirts.
smoke plumed
high in the sky.
where were the sirens?
time counted,
but faltered indefinitely.
tears were shed
and memories branded
in that fateful
hour.

Torrents

the grey mist settles on the rich and needy
landscape and foliage, endearing the earth.
droplets of life amass and blanket the
unsuspecting world. a torrential downpour
unleashes streaks of light and sounds like
cymbals off in the distance. the saturated
ground becomes tiny pools; furrowing into
gullies, feeding streams and brooks and
flowing into vast bodies of wealth. the world,
filled with life, welcomes and thirsts
for this life-giving event.

Winter Storm

the wind driven whimsical, whirling
and wooly snowflakes surprise and
surrender to the grateful ground.
the air amassing flakes to a blizzard,
salting and peppering the earth, becoming a
white-snowy covering. birds and animals
hastening to their heartfelt homes,
a myriad of footprints swallowed up by
the ongoing blizzard. the storm is beginning to subside.
sunset dances and displays a tranquil and peaceful
picture of a winter wonderland. the surreal
sky is overcome by the starry and
shining winter dream-state. the earth beckons for a
new virgin view of the world,
for enjoyment and effluent love
toward land and life.

One Day

the birds eagerly and excitedly
flock to the remnants of feed littered
at the base of a tall feeder. each gathers and collects
the morsels, satisfying but segregating
without sharing any amount generously among
themselves. white butterfly drifts along,
flitting and fluttering with no rush or
hurried signals. white and grey rabbit
wanders into the green foliage of young
vegetables and yellow and red flowers.
he nibbles at the base and leaves of some
lettuce stalks planted near the feeder.
the sky is clear blue. the sun climbs to the
pinnacle of the day and slowly slides
down as the afternoon passes by. often a hawk or
lone eagle sails by in the vertical troughs of heated air,
buoyed by the pressure differences amassed in the sky
created in the form of upward and downward drafts.
night settles in, while the stars light up the sky
and nocturnal life gradually emerges.

Bird's Haven

the bottomless bird bath's bright and golden sheen
reflects the golden sun rays back to a perching sparrow.
the bold breast casts a bright orange sheen
rather than the bird's black and bluish breast like
the veil that enshrouds life.
overcoming the blackness of the veil
begins with the basic affirmation of living and believing;
capable of forgiving yourself
and possessing the capacity of loving yourself and another.
we celebrate and call forth all our love for God.
the sounds of birds chirping from beautiful
branches of distant trees amplifies with
each voice like a melodic and harmonious
choir. the peacefulness of the bountiful
days mirrors the time given to us while each day and
hour becomes a measuring stick by the Hand of
blossoming eternity.

Watery Dwelling

storm subsides leaving
    traces of electrical activity
        and distant thunder.

long legged black and white
    egret strides watery shallows,
        trekking homeward bound.

water laps against shore;
    beaver drags felled forage
        back to submerged lair.

loon calling his mate,
    as if serenading her
        under moon and stars.

mottled osprey nestles young,
    staring down at sheer heights
        atop abandoned wooded pylon.

dawn arrives;
    perchance a rainbow appears,
        sun rears its head with splendor.

Nature's Calling

the intoxicating lustrous land leaves an imprint of
lasting beauty, branding and baring itself to the
beholder. the wondrous waves, wrestling within a
wealthy body of bluish-green, cresting and later
crashing upon the craggy lonesome landscape
dotting the jagged and crooked coastline. the majestic
mountains transform and tower with piercing precipices
hanging on the horizon; touching the serenity of the bold
and bluish sky. the winding and whimsical river, flowing
and forcing its imprint on the sandy shoreline; removing
sediment from its eroding walls and widening water basin.
the luscious land shapes and shades the valley situated
between the roaring river and the mile-high mountains.
the stupendous sun is shining and radiating its rays on the
awesome all-inspiring glorious globe of a world called
earth.

Ole's Ball Game

the fans collect at the ticket booth,
waiting to be a part of the game.
suddenly the ball leaves the bat,
its flight unknown,
until possibly caught by an out-fielder
or perhaps to enter the fan's domain.
the seventh inning stretch creates
opportunities, for both teams
and fans alike, to rest and regroup.
the highs of the sport
are similar to life's triumphs
and the time given to each of us.
the game's outcome is not about
winning or losing,
but rather did you enjoy the game?

Tribute to a Fisherman

as the sun rises, dawn whispers its presence
and the morning beckons to us to reflect
and give thanks to God. the fisherman
counts his blessings as the day unfurls
and the anticipation heightens. tackle box,
 never far away, the rod and reel are collected up.
only moments away, bliss ten-fold
as he approaches his favorite spot. finally
the bait drawn, the culmination ends
at the end of the pole.

Ride N' Life

the resonance between the shifting hooves
beating of a horse and ride is not unlike
riding in an automobile with poor
shifting and suspension. the grace of the
ride is realizing the rider is an
extension of this beautiful beast,
broken down but still with a beckoning and
baby spirit. the life of this quad-legged
creature is not unlike the rider,
being born into this world and given life to
breathe and love and feed and die,
young or old in the span of time and
space given to us.

Wind-Scape

the beautiful and billowy breeze neither
stays nor goes but remains in each moment
with peaceful and tranquil feelings
imparting love. partitions, like a slide
show, slicing and freezing time and space.
they exist differently from forthcoming
frame on frame of moment to moment
infused with love.
the flowers blossom and
beckon in the breeze, bending and
twisting but neither breaking or
changing as each moment passes by.
love flourishes as the onlooker
looks deeply into Nature.

Loosely Quarried

have you ever been in a quandary about
your next situation, like being trapped in a
large quarry? mindful of the mines scathing
the scenery, watchful of the warnings and
dangers of the deepening and dark holes in the
decimated ground. where malevolent machinery
lives and loosens the earth of its riches and leaves
only leftover rubbish. people riddle the land,
depriving the world in the name of progress and
prosperity; pillaging as they go, devouring the
glorious earthen soil and glistening waterways in
the name of greed and power. lining pockets
and purses of an elite and evil twisted minority
of dull and dimwitted power hungry degenerates.

Walk in the Park

strolling by the riverside, the call of nature
beckons to all onlookers. trees and grass
cover and carpet the rolling hills in a velvety
royal green, shielding the woodland animals
lurking about. sky dazzles and hypnotizes
the surroundings with beautiful white silhouettes.
the light, filtering and cascading
down through the line of firs, and mirroring itself upon
the glassy waters. serenity careens gently upon the soul
and the peacefulness is tasted by all who participate
in the wonderland free for all.

Sojourn Journey

morning comes early and gazing
about camp, crimson and white
are drawn in, clothed in yellow and green,
shades of manifestations of heavenly delight.
the magnificent firs arch themselves
to the sky while being lost
in reverence to the seas of blue.
the sun raises its mighty hand
and shines deeply on all living creatures.
a breath-taking view of the waters
crowns the memory by you,
the artist.

Thirsty-Earth

the earth's spirit thirsts for a deep drink from the
heavens, as the clouds burst open and offer
droplets, magically pouring down
in streams of consciousness from Mother
Nature. the dark green foliage, trees and
shrubs, are blanketed by the rich life-giving
process; enlivening through moisture to
saturate and fill the flowing bodies of wealth
and quench the inner drought of the
earthen soil. the ground beckons to the sky
in earnest and benevolent whispers,
perchance a rainbow is painted, arching
across from horizon to horizon.

Celebrate

seasons magically resound and resonate
as time drifts by of its own accord.
music of life flows and offers hope and peace.
a bystander has only to see and feel and give his
heart to each moment. one is seeking in each
opportunity a relationship of sharing
and caring with other people.
days float by like white puffy billowy
moments of magic. the sun playing hide
and seek as the exchange of light and darkness
covers the earth, manifesting itself in
beauty and boldness.

New Earth

the song birds return as winter releases
its hold on the barren earth. springtime
offering life new possibilities as buds,
seeds and enlivening foliage remake and
reawaken the new earth. a new enriching
green emerges and takes hold as God
breathes life into the world once more.
the beauty transforming the world as one
looks with inner gratitude and with
complete enjoyment, seeing past the veil
of mystery shrouding everyday life.
remember to keep a heart full of
love and laughter, sharing and caring as
your path takes you through the world.

Rain N' Shine

the raindrops falling, sending the wild
life scurrying about to their secure
secret sanctuaries. the frequency
of the drop, ever increasing and racing
to the ground is like an artist's
canvas stretching to the breaking limits.
the ground becomes saturated with
dime-size fists of ice littering the earthen
soil's surface. the sun is rallying and beckoning
at day break with shining arms like dual
rainbows, beaming at the beholder as the
enamoring sky of love nestles in his heart.

V

SPIRITUAL WORKS

"To love is to believe, to hope, to know;
Tis an essay, a taste of Heaven below."

-Edmund Waller

Earth-scape

blue veil littered and layered with
white billowy puffs of moments and
motion. blossoming firs arching
skyward toward the sun and stars.
landscape launches and defines
strength with beauty while melding
with the bold horizon. dwellings
mottle the hillside as seen from
the eye of an eagle soaring high
overhead. the vast bodies of
water glisten like an emerald dancing
between the sun and the hills. the sun silhouettes
the valley like a stilled motion picture,
frame by frame drawn across the scenery.
the craggy canyon creates
a rainbow of colors like a revolving
prism with the shimmering sunlight
casts a picture of delight.

Stars' Haven

the stars and planets are a picture perfect to a
panoramic portal; a bright and blinking
sea of lights like a continuous out-cropping
of flashing cities. twilight darkness replaces the wispy
veil of cloud cover, which in turn is overcome by total
duskiness. the starlight streams down upon the smooth
surface of a lake; glowing less luminously than the
super lovely setting moon shining over the same lucent
body of water. the nighttime sky vibrates between the
stars and planets, as a celestial view is courted
by a vigilant person.

Rich N' Redeeming

the rich and redeeming qualities
of life are forever knocking at one's
heart strings. a harp musically
and masterfully in-tune.
nature playing-out her story. the music
soars and skyrockets, overcoming the
blue radiating sky. colliding with the
opaque and oppressive clouds hanging
and harboring near-by. the peaceful and
pleasant feeling enlivens and empowers
one to enjoy and enter the rich and
redeeming qualities of life. the circle of
life is foretold and forthcoming.

Heart to Heart

the radiating and revolving
light of gold masterfully, mindfully and
meticulously renders itself to all
colors and creeds embellishing this
exciting earth. nature entwines and
envisions, redeems and receives
the enjoyment and enthralling days.
moments are measured and
metrically realized. the dreams
and distance achieved is richly and remotely
realigned by the dominion of the spirit
when pondering the mystery and
miracle of life.

Starry-Night

the colossal clouds congregate
the sea-borne sky, like stacking and
staggering ships organized
and orderly. the surreal sky is decorated
by a delivering and demonstrating
sunset courting the heartfelt
horizon. the onset of twilight
offers a slight reprieve to the
senses before reaching for a
starry session of stars' delight.
the world revolves and
rotates, rendering a heart-to-heart
revelation. the perfect and
pulsating sky deepens while
an acute awareness opens outwardly and
extends endlessly.

Star Burst

day trickles by.
the clouds change tempo
as the blue zooms in and out
of consciousness. the world
cruises on auto-pilot,
oblivious to the life-giving and abounding
transformations ongoing.
the sun bursts through the scenery,
casting its image on the ground.
the golden orb leaves an indelible mark,
stretching beyond itself,
creating a picture of beauty
as it melds with God's creation.
as the earth spins,
moments passby,
with sharing and enriching hearts
and spirits intertwined forever.

Christmas Cheer

bells and bows,
raising eyebrows as boxes pile up
under the lighted tree.
the view is engaging and enthralling,
under the watchful eyes of all children
of all sizes and ages. merriment of
Christmas permeates each of us and makes us
joyous and jaunty, enlivening feeling
as we honor our God and pass the peace of joy
to one another.

Promise Land

time evolves both perfunctory and perplexing.
the day runs its course, plunging wildly
and whimsically following its own golden string
strewn along the pre-laid path. the path bumps and
bounces over the land affecting the course but
not the ride. experiencing but not misleading,
the golden string moves one over the crooks and valleys
through mountainous terrain, offering spiritual
growth and renewal. the earth, in spoonful-
by-spoonful samplings of pure bliss, transforms and
transfixes naked and dormant fir into life-giving
moments of shooting buds and displays of
greenery. a stout and dapple forming birch has life
coursing through the trunk and branches.
the miracle of life remains a mystery
but forever is embedded in the living land promised
by God.

Coffee for Two

the coffee shop overfilling and ringing
with mirth and memorable conversation.
floating and finding ownership in the
nooks and crannies of the enclosed room.
no longer smoke but steam
spent words between friends and strangers alike.
the loneliness cuts through and severs the
moments like a dark dagger formed out of
the thick fog offered up by the grand
imagination of nature. the hunger for
life is measured by ones own cravings
and constitution to offer themselves up to
the magical moments we have with each other.

Poetic Warfare

poetry is a weapon, and should be used,
to battle in the world's literary trenches.
creative juices, flowing like molten lava,
singeing and wreaking havoc in the world.
fighting reaches a climax,
challenging and calling forth
armored metaphors and shielded similes.
air saturated with poetic cadence,
poem rips and tears
holes in the fragile fabric of reality.
stillness continues yielding
a silent message from the tangible.

"the first and last lines" by John Montague

Shangri-La

sun casting and crowning,
radiating and redeeming,
focusing and framing. there are
snapshots of surreal and star-studded coloration
upon the changing canvas.
life is captivating and claiming,
invoking and immersing the self
within the tapestry of threads.
clouds passing like mottled
off-white sails in a cascading sea of blue.
wind soaring and singing.
essence of life tasting and touching;
marriage between heaven and earth.
twist of the dial, the starry heaven.
witnessing and wishing,
seeking and showing.
beauty beckoning and bombarding the earth.
musical melodies erupting,
twinkling and throbbing.
pulsating stars, planets, quasars, galaxies and
black holes endlessly and eternally
engulf and extend,
freeing the human spirit.

Testimony

the blanketing and beckoning cloud cover
serenely casts a sublime and eerie backlight before the
storm gives rise to release a torrent of raindrops.
the pounding and parading moisture saturates and sends
a message to the earthen soil, satisfying foliage, fowl
and animals alike. the releasing and riveting rain
motions and moves, seeks and showers, creating new
landscapes. small brooks and streams garnish new life
as the water gains abundant nutrients and disperses to
all life for survival. water, the essence for all creatures,
continues and creates, invoking and immersing the
newness of life.

Star's Delight

starlight falls and covers us in a transcendental
mind-meld with His delight. our destiny is marked
by the light in our lives as we live out our dreams in
pulsating and precious moments. the light in our
dreams steers us through the crooks and valleys as we
deepen our life's values and essence in living.
the sky and yonder blue are limitless as our lives
unfurl and we enliven and bask in the light. the light in
our hearts and souls direct the path we take to shape
and frame ourselves in the image of our Creator.

Swirl N' Dance

autumn leaves swirl and dance
when a gentle breeze chooses and
regards the fallen heroes. the colors
of the day permeate the trees, as the
sun filters through the jungle of leaves.
squirrels decorate the flooring of the earth,
unsettling leaves to hide their prize.
a variety of birds reside in branches,
thickets and thatched nests,
living and singing in harmony with
nature. the world is in constant flux;
the fall leaves and colors leave a
memory pushing one forward.

Biography

Steven Jacobson was born in the Midwest in LaCrosse, WI. He attended UW-LaCrosse completing a double major in Physics and Abstract Mathematics. Subsequently, he relocated to the Twin Cities. Steven has published his poetry in national and international magazines and on-line sources. He has attended the Loft Literary Center. He enjoys writing about Nature and children, expounding on the spiritual essence of the subject.